WOODLAND Wonder

6 sample pages

2 sets of 24

Jen Racine coloring book pages!

instagram: @jenracinecoloring

facebook.com/jenracinecoloring

www.jenracine.com

BOOKS BY JEN RACINE

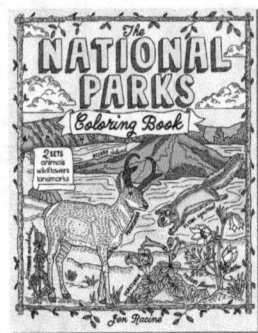

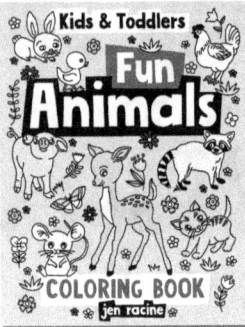

ETSY SHOP
www.etsy.com/shop/jenracinecoloring

Copyright © 2019 by Eclectic Esquire Media LLC
Published by Lake George Press

ISBN: 978-1-951728-00-7

No part of this publication may be reproduced, distributed or transmitted in any form or by any means, without the prior written permission of the publisher, except in the case of brief quotations embodied in critical reviews and certain other noncommerical uses permitted by copyright law.

SAMPLE PAGE FROM

GARDEN GNOMES COLORING BOOK

© JEN RACINE

SAMPLE PAGE FROM

THE NATIONAL PARKS COLORING BOOK

© JEN RACINE

SAMPLE PAGE FROM

I LLOVE LLAMAS COLORING BOOK

© JEN RACINE

SAMPLE PAGE FROM

ASTROLOGY CATS COLORING BOOK

© JEN RACINE

SAMPLE PAGE FROM

I LOVE MERMAIDS COLORING BOOK

© JEN RACINE

SAMPLE PAGE FROM

I LOVE MAGICAL ANIMALS COLORING BOOK

© JEN RACINE

www.ingramcontent.com/pod-product-compliance
Lightning Source LLC
Chambersburg PA
CBHW080026130526
44591CB00037B/2690